Derbyshire's Canals
Bert Clarke

Point where the Derby Canal (foreground) joined the Erewash Canal above Sandiacre Lock.

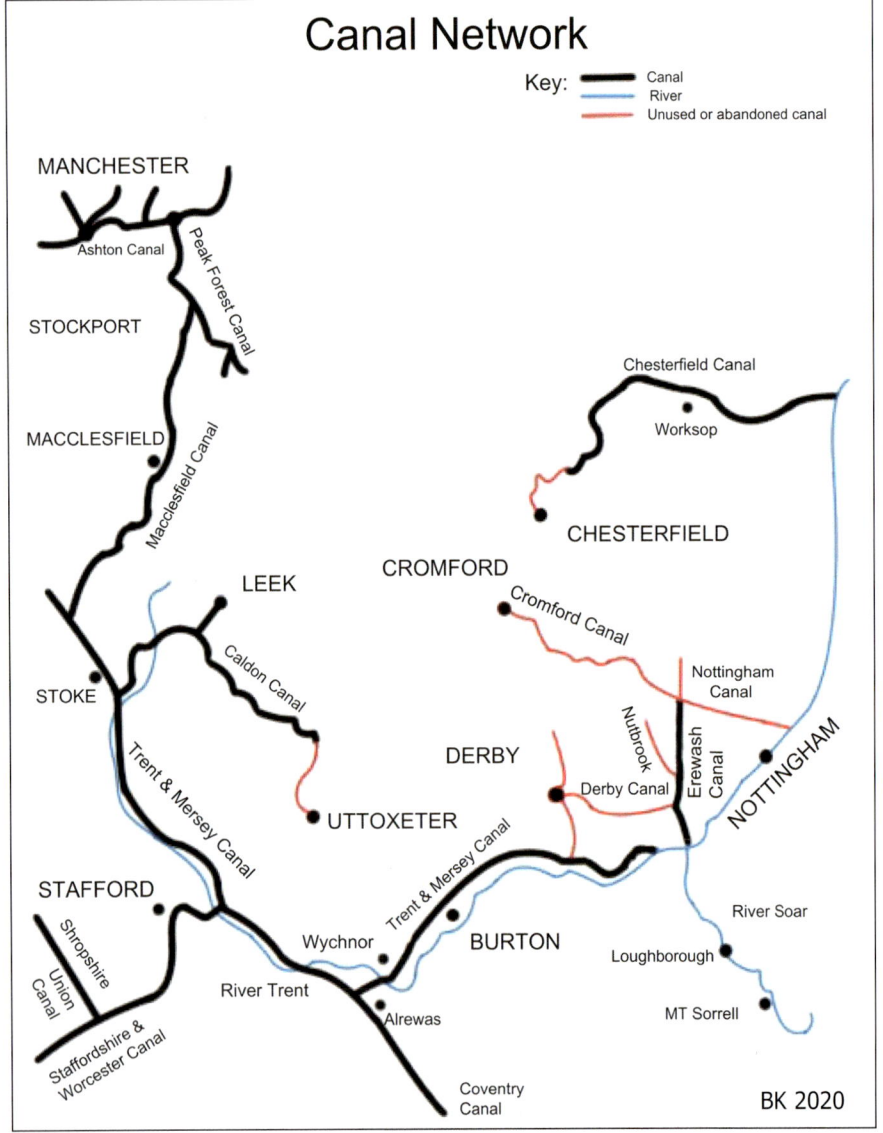

© Bert Clarke, 2020
First published in the United Kingdom, 2020,
by Stenlake Publishing Ltd.
www.stenlake.co.uk
ISBN 978-1-84033-829-4

The publishers regret that they cannot supply
copies of any pictures featured in this book.

Printed by
P2D Books, 1 Newlands Rd,
Westoning, Bedford, MK45 5LD

One of the flight of 15 locks at Thorpe Salvin.

Introduction

The seven canals of Derbyshire are a unique part of our heritage. What remains of them serve as reminders of a bygone age. Canals were a natural and progressive development of river improvements and can best be described as 'artificial water channels for transport purposes, built to connect places hitherto inaccessible by water'. Land-locked Derbyshire lies 60 miles from the sea with its only link, prior to the canal age, being provided by the River Trent, that great water highway of the North Midlands, which loops round the southern half of the county on its long journey of 170 miles to the Humber Estuary and the North Sea.

The English canal network was developed over a period of 74 years from 1761 to 1835 and it was during this time that all seven of the Derbyshire canals were constructed in the 31 years from 1774 – 1805 to play their part in the Industrial Revolution. In view of its importance as a means of transportation the Trent was the 18th century equivalent of the M1 motorway and six of the canals were connected it Trent in some form.

This book sets out to explain when, where, how and by whom the canals were built and for what purposes. Derbyshire at that time was rich in mineral wealth and had many cotton-spinning mills powered by water. The various routes, difficulties encountered and engineering works of note are described, together with descriptive details of the countryside through which they pass, which is delightful in many parts.

The heyday of the canal age is now long past but five of the original seven still exist. Havens of peace and tranquility they wind their way through the English countryside like linear parks where boating, walking, fishing and observing wildlife can all be enjoyed.

James Brindley and the Trent and Mersey Canal

With regard to canal history Derbyshire can lay claim to the double distinction of being the birthplace of James Brindley, the first of our great canal engineers, who was responsible for the survey and construction of its first canal, the Trent and Mersey. This long waterway, 93.5 miles in length, passes through the counties of Cheshire and Staffordshire before arriving in Derbyshire. Brindley was a largely self-taught genius of humble origins, born in 1716 at Tunstead in Derbyshire – a remote upland hamlet in the parish of Wormhill, near Buxton, which was, and indeed still is, nothing more than a few scattered farms. His birthplace was a wayside cottage, long since demolished, but the enclosed plot of ground on which it stood, known as 'Brindley's Croft', still exists with the site being marked with an inscribed plaque. In nearby Wormhill an impressive monument has been erected in his memory.

When aged 17 Brindley entered into an apprenticeship as a millwright and wheelwright at Sutton near Macclesfield, where it soon became apparent that he had a natural aptitude for such work, which he took to with great enthusiasm. The millwrights of those times were our first engineers who built wind and water mills. Working mainly in wood to construct the water wheels, mill sails and the gearing which

James Brindley

The Brindley Memorial, Wormhill.

Above: **Approach channel to Trent and Mersey from the Trent.**
Right: **In the foreground is the approach channel to the canal, whilst in the centre the Derwent meets the Trent.**

drove them, the skills of the blacksmith, stonemason and builder were also called for with their dams and sluices, wheel pits and water courses. Such work being carried out under supervision of the millwright. Upon completion of his apprenticeship Brindley moved to Leek in Staffordshire where he set up in business on his own account. Being an ambitious and industrious young man he soon had his sights set on the Potteries which was then a hive of industrial activity and in 1750 he set up a workshop there. This brought him into contact with many of the local landowners and manufacturers, one such group being headed by Earl Gower of Trentham, who were considering the feasibility of constructing an artificial waterway – as canals

Joining the Trent from the Trent and Mersey.

were then called – to link the ports of Liverpool and Hull in order to facilitate a much improved mode of transport for the pottery and china manufacturers of north Staffordshire and the salt producers of Cheshire. Canals were not a British invention as they had been in existence on the Continent for many years, particularly in southern France where the Canal du Midi dates from 1666. Nearer to home the St. Helen's Canal, 10 miles in length and built to carry coal from the St. Helen's coalfield in Lancashire to the River Mersey, was proving to be a profitable concern and had attracted widespread interest since opening in 1757.

Derwent Mouth Lock
– start of the Trent and Mersey.

Boats moored at Shardlow.

Clock Warehouse, Shardlow — now a pub and restaurant.

It was a huge and ambitious undertaking, fraught with difficulties, but despite this, in 1758, Brindley was engaged to survey and plan a route. This was to be his major achievement as with remarkable foresight he envisaged that it would eventually form the basis of a network of canals linking up the four main rivers of the country – Trent, Mersey, Severn and Thames – and he was proved right. Brindley referred to it as his 'Grand Cross' scheme, so called as it resembled in outline the cross of St. Andrew (X), with each of the four rivers representing an arm of the cross. In 1762, whilst working on the survey, he met his future wife, Anne, then a girl of 16. Three years later they were married, Anne then being 19 and Brindley 49!

The survey took eight years to complete, an Act of Parliament was secured, and on 26th July 1766, the Staffordshire potter, Josiah Wedgwood, cut the first sod at Burslem. It was a colossal undertaking on a scale hitherto unknown and 11 years were to pass before it was finally completed in 1777. From a connection with the Bridgewater Canal at Preston Brook it runs in a south-easterly direction for 67 miles to Fradley

Shardlow Lock.

The Trent and Mersey approaching Swarkestone.

Junction, there turning to the north-east for the remaining 26.5 miles to the Trent. The canal had 76 locks, five tunnels, 160 aqueducts and 213 road bridges, and just north of the Potteries lay the greatest engineering problem by far, the driving of a tunnel through Harecastle Hill. At just over one and a half miles in length 11 years were to pass before it was finally completed. It lay along the summit level, or the highest point above sea level of the canal, and once through it locks down through Stoke-on-Trent and into the Trent Valley, which it follows for the remainder of its journey. Just beyond Burton-on-Trent it arrives in Derbyshire by crossing the River Dove on a long, low aqueduct of 12 arches. The remaining 14 miles lie within the county and pass through a truly delightful landscape of farmland and the canalside villages of Willington, Findern, Swarkestone, Weston, Aston and Shardlow, all of which add greatly to its charm.

Shardlow, one mile from the Trent, became the transhipment point where cargo from the much larger Trent barges was transferred to the traditional 70-foot canal narrow boats. Large warehouses were built for storage

Stenson Lock, south of Derby.

Stenson Lock, south of Derby.

The canal at Stenson.

Derbyshire section of canal just beyond aqueduct at Dove Bridge.

purposes, along with wharves and bays to facilitate the mooring, unloading and loading of boats. Stables were built to accommodate the many towing horses. Cargo of all descriptions poured in – coal, limestone, gypsum, iron, lead, pottery and china, timber, salt, malt, barley, beer and cheeses. It became an inland port of great importance, humming with life and bustling with activity, and was a great meeting place for the many canal and river boatmen who arrived there. Alas, with the decline in trade due to the arrival of the railways all such activity is now long gone, but many of the old buildings still remain. There is a boat-building yard and two large marinas to cater for the vast increase in leisure cruising. The canal joins the Trent at the Derwent Mouth, so-called as just a few yards downstream that river flows in from Derby. From this point the Trent is navigable for 114 miles to the Humber Estuary and the North Sea.

Aqueduct across the Dove, near Willington.

Brindley was what is now termed a 'workaholic', as between 1758 and 1772, a period of 14 years, he carried out the survey of no less than 19 canals and it was while working on the last of these in 1772, the Caldon (a branch of the Trent and Mersey), that tragic consequences were to result. Whilst thus engaged he got soaked to the skin in a sudden downpour and became seriously ill, his condition being aggravated by diabetes and overwork. These factors resulted in his early death on 27th September 1772, at the age of 56. His is remembered today in the name of several streets, schools, an arts centre and a couple of pubs.

Other canals were to follow, six in total, but this was the first. It transformed the landscape and resulted in a much improved and vast increase in trade and proved to be a highly profitable waterway, with its £100 shares rising in value to a peak of £2,400, with huge dividends for its shareholders, a sample of such being:

1810	40%
1811	45%
1813	50%
1821	75%
1824	75%
1829	75%

Opened throughout in May 1777, the Derbyshire section was opened five years earlier in 1772, and still remains thus, having taken on a new lease of life for leisure cruising.

The Peak Forest Canal and Tramway

The Peak Forest Canal and its extension tramway are unique in a number of respects: it was the last of the Derbyshire canals; was the only one to penetrate the area of high moorland in the north-west of the county; and was planned to run at two separate levels, with the locks concentrated in one flight at its centre. In 1791 the idea of a canal was discussed by local landowners seeking an improved mode of transport for limestone and lime, then much in demand for building and agricultural use in Cheshire, Lancashire and Yorkshire. In the Manchester area were many cotton mills and this important industry sought improved transport for imports of raw cotton and the export of cotton goods. As a consequence, in 1793, Thomas Brown, a local surveyor, was engaged to survey a suitable line from the Ashton Canal, at Dukinfield, to the limestone quarries at Dove Holes which he completed that year.

Bugsworth Basin — view of main bay from the south.

Bugsworth Basin – with the Navigation Inn on the left.

His proposal was in four parts: a level stretch of seven miles; a long flight of locks up into the high ground; a level stretch of six and a half miles; and a tramway extension of five and a half miles up into the quarries, the total distance being 20 miles. A second opinion was sought from Benjamin Outram (engineer of the Cromford Canal), who was also commissioned to supply an estimate of costs. He modified the plans slightly and supplied an estimate of £115, 794. A public meeting to promote the scheme was then held at the Ram's Head, Disley, on 5th December 1793, which met with favourable response. An Act was applied for and obtained in 1794 and Outram was appointed chief engineer, with Brown as his assistant. Work began in June,

Bugsworth Basin – mooring bay.

Bugsworth Basin – at the foot of the tramway.

Bugsworth Basin where an old crane support column still stands at the foot of the tramway.

1794, at various points along the surveyed route, and the first section to be completed was the upper level above the proposed lock flight and its tramway extension. Both were completed in August 1796. This stretch runs for six and a half miles by way of Strines, Disley, New Mills and Furness Vale to its terminal basin at Bugsworth from where the tramway climbs 401.5 feet over the course of five and a half miles by way of Whitehough, Bridgeholme Green, Chapel Milton, Chapel-en-le-Frith and Barmoor Clough to the quarries. Just short of the basin a short branch of a half-mile was dug to Whaley Bridge. This high level section is known as the 'Upper Peak Forest Canal'.

Work was also underway along the lower stretch of seven miles from Dukinfield to Marple which runs level by way of Hyde, Woodley and Romily, beyond which it passes through a tunnel of 308 yards at Hyde Bank, followed by one of 176 yards at Butterhouse Green and a third of 100 yards at Rosehill, which no longer exists as the roof was later removed and it was converted into a cutting. Marple marks the end of this stretch. It was here that the first of the two major engineering problems was encountered – the crossing of the deep and steep-sided valley of the River Etherow. This was achieved by the construction of Marple Aqueduct, an impressive structure of red sandstone, 80 feet in height at its centre, with an overall length of 368 feet which carries the water channel over the valley on three arches, each of 56 feet span with the river being confined to the central arch. It took five years to build and was completed in November, 1799. Most unfortunately it is now difficult to fully

Starting point of the former Peak Forest Tramway at Bugsworth Basin.

End of the Whaley Bridge arm of the Peak Forest Canal.

From the top of Marple Locks a narrowboat leaves the Peak Forest to join the Macclesfield Canal.

appreciate its scale and form as the valley is heavily wooded at this point and much of the structure is screened by trees. This section, ending with the aqueduct, is known as the 'Lower Peak Forest Canal'.

There was at this point two completed sections of canal, separated by a distance one mile over the course of which the level rose by 209 feet, thereby presenting a formidable obstacle to be overcome. It was proposed to bridge this gap by the construction of a flight of 16 locks but the financial resources of the canal company were insufficient and so, as a temporary measure until the necessary funds could be raised, an inclined tramway was laid to connect the two levels. It remained in place for six years. In 1803 a loan of £24,000 was forthcoming from Sir Richard Arkwright, the

Upper section of Marple Locks.

Lower section of Marple Locks.

Cromford mill owner, enabling them to go ahead. The flight was completed two years later in October, 1805, when the canal became fully navigable, the end result being 14½ miles of canal and five and a half miles of tramway. A considerable supply of water was necessary to operate the flight of locks and this came from a large reservoir constructed by the canal company at Coombes, near Chapel-en-le-Frith. Situated above the summit level it lies at some distance from the canal, with the water flowing along a feeder channel two miles in length. Covering an area of 45 acres the reservoir is 50 feet deep and has a retaining wall in the form of an earth dam 1,000 feet in length. Despite this it soon proved to be insufficient and so in 1831 a second reservoir was built at Todd Brook.

It took 11 years to complete this waterway at a cost of £177,000, well in excess of Outram's estimate of £115,794. In 1831 it was joined at the top of Marple Locks by the

Marple Aqueduct over the River Etherow.

Macclesfield Canal, which arrived from its junction with the Trent and Mersey at Kidsgrove. That same year the Cromford and High Peak Railway arrived from the Cromford Canal to connect with the upper level at Whaley Bridge. Limestone, lime and cotton was the principal traffic. During the 19th century some 600 tons of limestone and lime were being despatched daily from Bugsworth Basin in a fleet of 40 narrowboats, which returned with coal, raw cotton, vegetables and a variety of general merchandise. It was in continuous operation until 1925 when the tramway closed, thus depriving the canal of its major source of traffic, which was now being transported by the railway network. However, it was not allowed to wither and die; a restoration programme was initiated and it still remains fully navigable to its splendid complex basin at Bugsworth, its name being taken from the nearby village, formerly of that name, which in 1930 was renamed Buxworth at the instigation of the villagers who objected to the unsavoury nature of its former name which was retained for the basin.

This is a delightful waterway, for the most part rural, passing through an area full of historical interest. The lock flight is situated amidst a wooded landscape and blends in well with its surroundings. The upper level is a haven of peace and tranquility as it winds its way high along the western slopes of the Goyt Valley, which is both broad and deep so that the river lying far below is rarely seen. From the left bank the land falls away into the valley, down tree-clad slopes and there are some fine far-distant views of the Pennine Chain. Furness Vale now has a large marina where boats can be seen from many parts of the country. This is a well-used canal, forming part of the 'Cheshire Ring', a circular cruising route of 97 miles taking in the Macclesfield, northern section of the Trent and Mersey, Bridgewater, Rochdale and Ashton canals and the Peak Forest to the top of Marple Locks. Long may it continue.

View north over Marple Aqueduct.

The Chesterfield Canal

The Chesterfield Canal was an early arrival on the canal scene, being the second of Derbyshire's seven canals. James Brindley was surveyor and engineer of this waterway, which ran for 46 miles from Chesterfield, by way of Worksop and Retford, to join the River Trent at West Stockwith. Plans for a canal had been discussed as early as 1768 as an improved means of transport was being sought by local landowners who wished to develop and expand coal deposits. Lead was also being mined in large quantities, much of which was exported down the Trent and there was a large ironworks at Staveley, near Chesterfield, which also sought improvements. The Trent was the main outlet but the difficulty lay in getting there as all

Start of the canal at Chesterfield from the right bank of the River Rother, which flows off to the left to fall over a weir.

Tapton Mill Bridge, Chesterfield, with a familiar landmark over the top.

Stretch near Tapton Lock, Chesterfield.

The canal at Staveley.

goods had to be sent overland by packhorse teams or horse and wagon, a slow and laborious process involving a journey of 24 miles to Bawtry, in South Yorkshire, where they were loaded onto boats and sent down the River Idle to the Trent.

In 1769 Brindley was engaged to survey a suitable line but as his services were much in demand he delegated the task to John Varley, one of his assistants. The survey met with Brindley's approval. Costs were estimated at £95,000 and in 1771 an Act of Parliament was secured and work commenced. East of Chesterfield the land slopes down into the valley of the River Rother, which marks the starting point of the canal. A channel was cut into the right bank which then winds its way along the river valley by way of Staveley, Renishaw and Killamarsh, to arrive at Norwood, 12 miles from Chesterfield, where a formidable problem presented itself in the form of the high and broad ridge of magnesian limestone which the canal had to cross. It did so by means of massive engineering works – a long tunnel and a total of 35 locks. At the Norwood (Chesterfield) end an impressive flight of 13 staircase locks

Starting point of the top flight of four staircase locks at Norwood, now derelict and concealed beneath a cloak of dense vegetation.

Foot of the flight of 13 staircase locks at Norwood, near Killamarsh.

was built to raise the water level – staircase locks are so-called as they resemble a staircase with the top gate of the first lock also acting as the bottom gate of the next one up.

The top of this flight marks the start of Norwood Tunnel – over one and a half miles (2893 yards) long and running dead straight it is 12 feet high, nine and a qurter feet wide and brick-lined throughout. A total of 3,000,000 bricks were used, made on-site as both the clay and the coal for firing were available locally. Work began in 1771 and was completed in 1775. The tunnel has no towpath and a one-way system was devised for the boats which were 'legged' through whilst the towing horses were led over the top. When Brindley died suddenly in 1772, his post of principal engineer was taken up by his brother-in-law, Hugh Henshall. The tunnel marks the start of the summit level, or highest point above sea level, of the canal, which runs for four miles and emerges at Kiveton Park in South Yorkshire where more locks were necessary to lower the level. Thorpe Locks, the first of these, is an impressive flight of 15 spread out over the course of a half-mile. Known locally as the 'Giant's Staircase' the flight contains two treble and two double staircases and is closely followed by the Turnerwood Locks, a flight of seven through which the canal falls to pass over a three-arched aqueduct

Western portal of the disused and abandoned Norwood Tunnel.

Above: **Summit level near Thorpe Locks.**
Left: **A delightful rural stretch of the canal along the summit level between Kiveton Park and Thorpe Locks.**

spanning the River Ryton and into Nottinghamshire. Thus, in slightly over one mile the canal has passed through 22 locks. Beyond the aqueduct the canal continues through Shireoaks, to Worksop, 20 miles from Chesterfield.

The remaining 26 miles of canal pass through pleasant, rural countryside and the towns and villages of Ranby, Retford, Clarborough, Hayton, Clayworth, and a tunnel 154 yards long at Drakeholes, Walkeringham and Misterton, to arrive at West Stockworth where it locks down into the Trent. Along this stretch are 15 locks all of which lower the water level. In the past West Stockworth was a river port of note but it now just caters for leisure craft. Water supply for the canal was by extraction from the River Rother at the Chesterfield end and by four reservoirs built above the summit level over Norwood Tunnel. The entire canal took just under six years to build at a cost of £150,000 (well above Brindley's estimate of £95,000) and was opened throughout on 4th June 1777. It proved to be of immense benefit and carried mainly mineral traffic consisting of coal, lead, stone, pottery and iron products from the Chesterfield and Staveley areas, also lime, timber, bricks, corn and agricultural produce from the more rural area of

Top of the flight of 15 locks at Thorpe Salvin, near Kiveton Park, South Yorkshire.

Journeys end at West Stockwith, where the canal joins the Trent.

the eastern end were also of importance and once established it enjoyed many years of modest prosperity, paying dividends of between 6% and 8% and its £100 shares rose to a peak of £150. Imports of foreign wheat came up the Trent in stoutly built Humber keels, which were termed 'dumb boats' as they had neither mechanical nor horse power and sailed beneath a square-rigged sail. At West Stockwith the grain was transhipped into narrow boats and conveyed to flour mills at Worksop.

The canal's most notable cargo was the magnesian limestone extracted from quarries at North Anston, two miles north of the canal in South Yorkshire, which was used to rebuild the Houses of Parliament following a fire which completely destroyed them in 1834. This is a fine-grained, honey-coloured stone, 250,000 tons of it were shipped down the canal from Kiveton Park, to the Trent, out into the North Sea, down the coast and up the Thames to Westminster. The canal continued to operate until 1907 when a large section of the roof caved in at the eastern end of Norwood Tunnel, completely blocking it and leaving a large crater in the field above. and resulted in its complete closure, together with the section westward to Chesterfield. The canal remained operational between Worksop and the Trent until 1955, when it was closed completely.

West Stockwith Lock and the River Trent.

This canal has many enthusiastic supporters and in 1968 the 26 mile stretch from Worksop to the Trent was re-opened. British Waterways have since restored the 22 locks at Turnerwood and Thorpe and boats can now navigate to the eastern end of Norwood Tunnel. In 1976 the Chesterfield Canal Society was formed with the aim of restoring the remaining 20 miles to Chesterfield. Work is continuing, with the main difficulties being restoration of the tunnel and the staircase locks at Norwood. It is possible to walk along the entire 46 miles of the canal along a long-distance footpath known as the 'Cuckoo Way'. The narrow boats along the canal were termed 'cuckoos' by the Trent boatmen who regarded them as inferior to the sturdy and far larger river boats, comparing them with the cuckoo's practice of laying its eggs in the nests of other birds to produce a bird of a different nature. This old waterway to the Trent has much of interest in relation to its route, architecture and the delightful and varied countryside and villages through which it passes, which is for the most part peaceful and secluded and far removed from the traffic-choked roads of the present age.

The Derby Canal

The Derby Canal could have been one of the first in the county but due to strong opposition from the proprietors of the Trent and Mersey and Derwent river navigations it was one of the last. In 1771 a proposal to incorporate it into the network then developing was made by James Brindley, by way of a canal from the Trent and Mersey to Derby and onwards to connect with the Chesterfield Canal. It was not proceeded with and 20 years were to pass before another proposal was forthcoming and Derby was completely cut off from the canal network, being by-passed by the Trent and Mersey and the Erewash canals. Derby had its river, the Derwent, which since 1721 had been navigable into the city from the Trent, a distance of 10 miles, but river navigations were unreliable as they were often impassable in parts due to summer droughts and winter floods.

Something needed to be done and decisive action was called for as the future prosperity of the town was being hampered by lack of a reliable and more efficient means of transport. The town frequently suffered from a shortage of coal, despite the fact that it was near at hand, but the problem was the slow and inefficient carriage by packhorse or horse and wagon, which were of limited value for heavy loads. A canal was seen as the

Starting point of former Derby Canal above Swarkestone Lock.

Derelict and overgrown bed of the canal towards Chellaston.

solution and this led to a meeting at the Bell Inn, Sadler Gate, in 1791. Support led to a second meeting in 1792, when a line of canal from the Trent and Mersey to Derby, and onwards to Little Eaton and Denby, was proposed to gain access to collieries at Denby, Horsley and Smalley and met with approval and a survey was commissioned.

Executed with remarkable speed and delivered the following month it recommended a link with the River Trent, at Swarkestone, to join and follow the Trent and Mersey Canal for a short distance to the top of Swarkestone Lock, there branching off north to Derby, crossing the Derwent by aqueduct and continuing northwards to Little Eaton and Denby, a total distance of 12.5 miles. Once over the aqueduct a branch of nine miles eastwards was also proposed to connect with the Erewash Canal at Sandiacre, with the total cost being estimated at £68,000. These proposals were modified in order to reduce costs and it was decided to end the canal at Little Eaton and complete the link to Denby by means of a horse-drawn

Long Bridge Weir across the Derwent at Derby.

Long Bridge across the Derwent at Derby.
courtesy Alwyn Davies

railway. The proposed aqueduct over the Derwent was also rejected in favour of an actual crossing of the river.

Early in 1793 an Act was applied for and obtained in May. Work began in August and the first sections to be completed were the railway extension of four and a half miles to Denby; the three-mile stretch of canal from Derby to Little Eaton, and the nine miles of canal from Derby to the Erewash, by way of Chaddesden, Spondon, Borrowash and Draycott, to join the canal above Sandiacre Lock, alongside which a tollhouse was built. All were operational by May, 1795.

It was not until this work had been completed that work on the five and a half mile Swarkestone – Derby section and the crossing of the Derwent was started early in June 1795. Crossing the river was the main engineering problem as it is 300 feet wide. As a first step a weir was constructed across it to secure a sufficient depth and constant supply of water and just above it,

Point where the former Derby Canal joined the Erewash Canal above Sandiacre Lock.

Line of the former Derby Canal, now filled in and converted into a footpath, just beyond the point where it joined the Erewash Canal.

slightly upstream, timber piles were driven into the river bed upon which a narrow timber bridge was built to enable the towing horses to cross whilst hauling the boats which crossed on the upstream side of the bridge which was fitted with a wooden fender to protect it from damage. It became known as 'Longbridge Weir'. From the north (Little Eaton) side of the river a short branch of a quarter mile was dug westwards to connect with the river to gain access to the Boar's Head cotton mills at Darley Abbey. The remaining section of five and a half miles was also dug from the top of Swarkestone Lock by way of Chellaston to Derby, with water being extracted from the Derwent so that no reservoirs were necessary. The last section, although not actually part of the Derby Canal, was a short branch of 600 yards connecting the River Trent with the Trent and Mersey Canal to enable the Trent river barges to reach Derby although this proved to be a failure as river traffic declined and the link was abandoned in 1817 and subsequently filled in. All this work was completed by 30th June 1796, when the canal became fully operational.

The canal was a broad navigation with lock chambers 90 feet long and 15 feet wide to accommodate the Trent barges of 14-feet beam. Once opened coal traffic

The toll house of the former Derby Canal which was built into the gable-end of the lock keeper's cottage at Sandiacre Lock.

increased substantially from 28,000 tons in 1798, to over 50,000 tons in 1803, which came down the Little Eaton branch, along with large quantities of stone for building purposes. It became a valuable and thriving concern for the town. Derby was at the hub of the system with traffic flowing in and out of the town from four different directions, with coal, building stone, corn, ironstone and lead being the main commodities carried, along with goods of all descriptions. Even passengers were catered for with a boat leaving Swarkestone each Friday morning bound for Derby Market. The final cost of construction amounted to £100,000, well in excess of Outram's revised estimate of £64,000, but the canal enjoyed many years of modest prosperity with its dividend payments being limited to 8%, with any profits in excess of this figure being used to reduce tolls.

In 1839 railways arrived in the town and gradually spread throughout the area but, quite remarkably, it was not until 1908 that decline set in with closure of the railway extension to Denby, followed by closure of the Derby-Little Eaton branch in 1935. Now deprived of its coal and stone traffic the canal struggled on but from 1945 onwards no commercial traffic was carried and in 1959 the 'long bridge' over the Derwent was demolished after being declared unsafe. All that now remains to mark its position is the weir. In 1961 a restoration plan was proposed but not acted upon and the end came in 1964 when it was completely abandoned and sections were sold off, built over or filled in and all that now remains are fragmented sections of the water channel at the Swarkestone end and along parts of the Derby – Sandiacre section. It was deserving of a better fate having served the town well during the 168 years of its existence.

In 1993 a volunteer group was formed with the aim of restoring it as a through navigation from the Trent and Mersey, at Swarkestone, to the Erewash, at Sandiacre, a distance of 14.5 miles, and a feasibility study declared that this was physically possible, economically feasible and environmentally desirable but the cost was estimated at £17.3 million pounds (well over £1 million pounds per mile), making it a daunting prospect so that if this aim is ever achieved it is likely to be in the long-term.

Erewash and Nutbrook Canals

Many of the early canals were extensions from rivers and the Erewash and its branch, the Nutbrook, fall into this category as both are extensions of the River Trent. The Erewash Valley lies in South Derbyshire and its heavy clay soil was rich in both coal deposits and ironstone. Throughout the 18th century many coal mines and ironstone workings were developed but expansion was hampered by the primitive methods of overland transport then available and colliery owners in particular were keen to expand and develop new markets by gaining access to the Trent, then the great water highway of the Midlands. James Brindley's work as surveyor and engineer of canals had not escaped their notice and as early as 1776 proposals were being made to cut a canal up the Erewash Valley and John Smith was engaged to survey a suitable line

His starting point was the north bank of the Trent, just below Sawley, at the now aptly named Trent Lock, situated just a short distance up-river from where the River Soar, flows in from Loughborough and Leicester, where

View of the River Trent from below Trent Lock on the Erewash Canal.

View south towards Trent Lock.

View north towards Long Eaton.

Long Eaton, a former textile town.

work was in progress to also make it navigable to the Trent. Smith's line runs northwards up the Erewash Valley, along the west bank of the river by way of Long Eaton, Sandiacre, Stanton Gate and Trowell, to Ilkeston and Cotmanhay, north of which it switches to the east bank which it follows to Langley Mill, where it terminates. It is 11.75 miles in length and spaced at intervals are 14 locks all of which raise the water level by 109 feet. No reservoirs were necessary as the River Erewash supplied all its requirements by way of feeder channels at Ilkeston Common and Langley Mill. Smith's survey was accepted by the promotors, who promptly applied for an Act of Parliament which they obtained in April 1777. John Varley, who had previously worked as Brindley's assistant on the Chesterfield Canal, was appointed chief engineer and work began. There were no great engineering difficulties and it progressed rapidly so that the canal was opened throughout in July 1779. The water channel was built to a width of 14 feet, six inches, in order to accommodate the Trent barges of 14 feet beam. Construction costs were a modest £21,000.

The Nutbrook Canal, a branch of the Erewash, was built to gain access to collieries at Shipley and West Hallam and ironstone workings. It was four and a half miles long and contained 13 locks which raised the water level by 82 feet. It left the left bank of the Erewash just above

Sandiacre Lock and lock-keeper's cottage.

Stanton Lock, five and three quarter miles from Trent Lock, and at its northern end three reservoirs were necessary to supply it with water. Opened in 1795 it was engineered by Benjamin Outram and cost £22,800 to build. Traffic increased substantially in 1846 when Benjamin Smith and his son, Josiah, built three blast furnaces and an iron foundry in order to take advantage of the rich ironstone and coal deposits of the area. Their works were positioned on the left bank of the Erewash, just above the point where the Nutbrook branches off, prospered to become the Stanton Ironworks Company in 1858.

On the Erewash coal was always the main commodity carried, Much of this went across the Trent and down the River Soar to Loughborough, along what was known as the Loughborough Navigation which had opened in 1778. The result was that by 1792, 70,000 tons was being carried annually and by 1829 this had risen to 170,000 tons. Other interconnecting canals were later built along its line, the first being its northern extension, the Cromford, which came in 1794, closely followed by the Nutbrook in 1795, and finally the Nottingham and the Derby in 1796. The Erewash became one of the most profitable canals in the country and in addition to coal it carried ironstone, iron, limestone, lead, millstones, gritstone, marble and chert. Upon reaching the Trent boats were able to navigate eastwards down the river to

Sandiacre Lock and former toll house for Derby Canal.

Pasture Lock, four and a half miles north of Trent Lock.

Boaters heading north from Stanton Lock.

Eastwood Lock, one and a half miles south of Langley Mill.

Gainsborough and Hull, westwards to the Trent and Mersey and southwards along the Soar to Loughborough, which by 1794 had been made navigable to Leicester and in 1814 along the Grand Union Canal to London. The Erewash was thus ideally placed at the centre of three major trading routes with a wealth of mineral deposits in its hinterland and these factors account for its huge success. Its profits were truly staggering as is indicated by the returns on its £100 shares:

1791	24%
1794	30%
1800	25%
1806	25%
1809	33%
1812	44%
1815	51%

These payments rose to a peak of 74% in 1825 and in 1840 64% was paid, This fell to 45% in 1841, and in the following 15 years it never fell below 21%.

Typical landscape along the northern section of the canal. Heanor is on the skyline.

The end of the Erewash and its interconnecting network was, like all other canals, eventually brought about by the spread of railways, and they were particularly hard-hit in 1847 when a line was opened up the Erewash Valley to Codnor Park which ran parallel to it and had many branch lines to collieries and other concerns along its route. The canal was robbed of much of its traffic and went into a process of slow decline with the end in sight. First to close was the Nutbrook Canal, where traffic ceased in 1895, apart from the lowermost half-mile which was retained by the Stanton Ironworks Company until that too closed in 1928. Next was the Nottingham Canal, where traffic also ceased in 1928, followed by abandonment in 1937. The Cromford Canal closed in 1944, and the following year the Derby Canal fell into disuse; it was abandoned in 1964. The Erewash survived the longest and was in use until 1952 and abandoned in 1964, but unlike the other four it was rescued by the Erewash Canal Preservation and Development Association, a local volunteer group. In partnership with British Waterways they have achieved their objectives and narrow boats can now navigate along its entire length.

Langley Mill Basin.

This well-preserved waterway is worthy of exploration. The first four miles pass through a largely urban environment but thereafter the views become more open and rural with fields, trees, hedgerows, low hills and distant spires. Along this stretch is Pasture Lock, a short distance beyond which the M1 motorway passes over the canal on a flyover, part of a distant world. Many of the locks at its northern end are delightfully situated and make for ideal picnic places. Not now being part of a through route, Langley Mill marks the end of the line and it is here necessary to turn round and go back. The local population appreciate their canal and make good use of it for their leisure activities: strolling along sections of the towpath, fishing, lazing, sunbathing, picnicking or just admiring the scenery.

The Cromford Canal

The Cromford Canal was an extension of the Erewash Canal, running for a distance of 14.5 miles to Cromford Meadows, where it terminated in Mill Lane, opposite the two cotton-spinning mills of Sir Richard Arkwright, the first of which opened in 1771, to secure its place in history as the first water-powered mill in the country, heralding the start of the Industrial Revolution. The Erewash and other canals had revolutionized inland transport so other landowners and manufacturers were keen to get in on the act and, collectively, had the financial resources to do so in order to expand and develop their coal and ironstone deposits along the upper Erewash Valley and the area around Ripley. Arkwright also required an improved mode of transport for the import of raw cotton and the export of cotton thread, which was being spun in huge quantities. However, it was Philip Gell of Hopton, a local landowner, who was the chief promoter and in 1787 he and other interested parties engaged William Jessop, a civil engineer of Newalk, to survey a suitable line. Jessop got to work and in 1788 produced his survey.

In 1789 an Act was secured, Jessop was appointed engineer, assisted by Benjamin Outram, a land surveyor and budding civil engineer of Ripley, who

Feeder channel at Cromford.

The canal near Cromford.

Former good shed and wharf at High Peak Junction where goods were transshipped from the canal onto the Cromford and High Peak Railway.

Leawood Pumphouse alongside the Derwent and High Peak Junction.

View over Wigwell Aqueduct towards Leawood Pumphouse.

was to act as superintendent of works. Langley Bridge Lock at Langley Mill marks the starting point and for the first four miles it climbed the gradual slope of the valley to Codnor Park. The canal had 14 locks and all were contained within this section, with seven spaced at intervals and a flight of seven at the top, which raised the water level by 82 feet. Beyond the top flight is a reservoir and the canal ran alongside this for a half-mile to the eastern portal of Butterley Tunnel. The reservoir marked the start of the long summit level of 10.5 miles and with its large storage capacity was ideally situated to supply the lower level with water. From its northern bank a short branch was dug to Pinxton, later extended to Mansfield by an eight-mile section of horse-drawn railway.

From the eastern end of Butterley Tunnel to Cromford was a 10-mile stretch of level canal. Driving of the tunnel was the first major engineering difficulty, to

penetrate the broad, high ridge dividing the Erewash and Amber Valleys. It ran dead straight and was just under one and three quarter miles in length. Some rock was encountered but the majority of the tunneling was through soft subsoils and seams of both coal and ironstone were encountered which were later worked and led to the formation of the Butterley Company. The tunnel was nine feet wide and eight feet high from the water surface, with a depth of five feet, designed to accommodate narrowboats of seven-feet beam. There was no towpath and the boats were legged through with a journey time of 90 minutes.

From the western end of the tunnel it is slightly over eight miles to Cromford. The canal emerges on the outskirts of Ripley to run through a long cutting enclosed by an overarching screen of trees and bushes which form a tunnel until the A610 is reached beneath which it is channeled in a culvert. Now in the Amber Valley it winds its way through Lower Hartshay to Buckland Hollow, there

Wigwell Aqueduct which spans the Derwent at High Peak Junction.

The short Gregory Tunnel some two miles from Cromford.

Another view of the short Gregory Tunnel.

passing through a short tunnel to run along the valley side on a ledge above the A610 by way of Sawmills to Bull Bridge, where the second major obstacle was encountered – the crossing of the valley. This was accomplished by the construction of Bull Bridge Aqueduct, a massive structure 200 yards long and 50 feet high which carried the canal over the A610 and the River Amber onto the west-facing slopes of the Derwent Valley, which it followed for the remaining six miles to Cromford. This is a most delightful stretch of waterway running high along the valley side above the River Derwent, which can be glimpsed down below from time to time. Much of the route passes through deciduous woodland, which is invested with an atmosphere of peace and seclusion. Beyond Whatstandwell it passes through a short tunnel, complete with towpath and timber handrail, to arrive at Leawood where a short branch of just under a half-mile heads off from the right bank to connect with a lead smelter, a cotton mill

Canal scene near Gregory Tunnel.

Typical scenery along the six mile stretch between Cromford and Ambergate.

Filled in section of the canal at Buckland Hollow Tunnel.

and stone quarries, but now only the cotton mill survives producing high quality knitwear. Just beyond the branch the third and last major problem was encountered – the crossing of the Derwent. This was achieved by the construction of Wigwell Aqueduct, an impressive gritstone structure 200 yards long and 30 feet high with a central arch of 79 feet spanning the river with a smaller arch on either side and above the keystone of the central arch, on the downstream side, is carved the date of its construction – 1792. Just one and a quarter miles beyond this point the end of the canal is reached at Cromford Wharf.

Water supply to the four-mile stretch of canal containing the 14 locks was by the reservoir at Codnor Park and also from Butterley Park Reservoir, built above the eastern end of the tunnel and reaching the canal by a stepped weir alongside the tunnel entrance. At Cromford it was received from the combined sources of an underground drainage sough and Bonsall Brook, the sough being the main supplier until it ran dry in in the 1840s when another sough was driven at a lower level. The canal company then constructed a steam-driven pumping engine alongside the aqueduct in order to extract water from the river. Opened in 1849 the gritstone engine

Section of water channel near Butterley Tunnel (Western End).

Butterley Tunnel (Western End).

house contains a massive beam engine with a piston 50 inches in diameter with a 10 feet stroke which enabled it to pump water from the river at the rate of 28 tons per minute (5,600 gallons) through a five feet diameter pipe which was built into the side of the canal below the water line. Now having been restored this engine can be seen 'in steam' at various times throughout the year.

Opened throughout in 1794, at a total cost of £83,055, almost twice that of Jessop's estimate of £42,697, many railways were built to connect it to collieries and ironstone workings and when the Butterley Company of Ripley came into existence in 1806 it carried a wide range of their products, including the iron framework supporting the huge canopy over the platforms at St. Pancras Station, which is in use to this day. In the 1820s plans were being made to extend it further north, to link with the Peak Forest Canal. This would have been a formidable undertaking for an area of high moorland lies between the two and a large number of locks would have been required, but there was an even greater problem, which in the end proved insurmountable, and that was an insufficiency of water across

Mileage plaque, Langley Mill Basin.

the high, and for the most part dry, intervening limestone plateau and so this proposal was abandoned and replaced by that of a rail link and the Cromford and High Peak Railway came into being. Opened in 1831 it ran for 33 miles to link the two. This remarkable early railway remained in existence for 136 years until closure in 1967.

The canal was a profitable venture and tonnages rose steadily to a peak of 320,517 in 1841, when a dividend of 20% was paid. Thereafter decline set in due to the spread of railways but in 1900 there was a serious subsidence in Butterley Tunnel, caused by mining operations beneath it, which resulted in its closure and it has never since reopened. Canal traffic did continue at either end until complete abandonment in 1944. It is unfortunate that this canal has not been restored as it is a most delightful waterway. In 1968 the aqueduct at Bull Bridge was completely demolished, thus making restoration even more difficult. The lower section containing the 14 locks is now almost completely obliterated, but the stretch up to the eastern end of the tunnel still remains, along with the water channel at the western end and in fragmented parts along to the now demolished aqueduct at Bull Bridge. However the best section is the six-mile stretch running from Cromford to Bull Bridge.

Langley Mill Basin – starting point of the canal.